# Fudge

## HOW THEY USED TO DO IT

Copyright © 2013 Two Magpies Publishing
An imprint of Read Publishing Ltd
Home Farm, 44 Evesham Road, Cookhill, Alcester,
Warwickshire, B49 5LJ

Commissioning Editor Rose Hewlett
Words by Sophie Berry
Design by Zoë Horn Haywood

All Images remain the copyright property of their respective owners, all attributions and copyright licences are referenced at the rear of the book.

This book is copyright and may not be reproduced or copied in any way without the express permission of the publisher in writing.

British Library Cataloguing-in-Publication Data A catalogue record for this book is available from the British Library.

# Contents

| | |
|---|---|
| Foreword | 1 |
| Introduction | 3 |
| History of Fudge | 7 |
| Story of the Store Cupboard | 11 |
| Wartime Rationing | 19 |
| Sourcing Your Supplies | 23 |
| Equipment | 27 |
| Measurements | 33 |
| ~ Cup Conversions | 36 |
| Temperature | 37 |
| ~ The Drop Test | 44 |
| Techniques | 45 |

# Contents

Recipes 51

~ Traditional Favourites 53

~ Classic College Recipes 67

~ Classic Twists 75

~ Wartime Recipes 85

The Etiquette of Serving 93

Gifts 97

# Foreword

*'Knowledge never learned in schools'*

*Watson, 1891*

The simple pleasure of mastering practical household skills has been all but forgotten over the last century. We live in an overly convenient, disposable world in which things arrive pre-packed, ready-wrapped and lacking in any craft, care, or quality.

It's time to reject this attrition of what were once everyday skills, time to get back to basics, time to remember How They Used To Do It.

The How They Used To Do It series will take you back to the golden age of practical skills; an age where making and mending, cooking and preserving, brewing and bottling, were all done within the home. The series will instruct you in a whole range of traditional skills that have fallen out of use, putting old knowledge into new hands. Using household items, nifty hints and tricks, and a little creativity you will be surprised what you can achieve.

The series has been carefully curated from a wealth of original resources to provide a wonderful blend of social history and practical instruction. The knowledge within these pages has been sourced from rare books, old newspapers and forgotten magazines to inform a whole new generation about How They Used To Do It .

# Introduction

## Introduction

# WELCOME TO THE WONDERFUL WORLD OF FUDGE MAKING.

# Introduction

With this little book in your hands you can turn even a humble kitchen into a hub of fudge-making activity, happily passing many a rainy afternoon creating mouth-watering treats. As well as lots of classic recipes this book is filled with fudge-making tips and techniques you can try as soon as you have mastered the basics.

What's more, you don't need lots of equipment or a vast array of ingredients to get started. Pleasingly, most of the equipment you will need will be found already tucked away in your cupboards and cutlery drawer.

# Introduction

The beauty of making your own fudge is that you can be sure to use the best and purest ingredients. In an age which tends to be increasingly synthetic, knowing exactly what has gone into your lovingly created confectionery is surely an attractive prospect.

Added to this, the result of fudge-making at home is often much thriftier than buying it ready made. By only making what you want, and in quantities you need, there is no waste.

# History of Fudge

# History of Fudge

Fudge is a soft, sweet confection made by carefully heating sugar, water and often milk or cream. The earliest mention of fudge was made in the late 1800s. A young lady called Emelyn Battersby Hartridge, who was a student at Vassar College in Poughkeepsie, New York mentioned fudge in a letter while she was a student.

She wrote that her school-mate's cousin made fudge in Baltimore, Maryland in 1886 and

## History of Fudge

sold it for 40 cents a pound. Emelyn managed to get hold of the fudge recipe, and in **1888**, made fudge for the Vassar College Senior Auction.

Word of Emelyn's fudge spread to other colleges which resulted in Wellesley and Smith having their very own versions of a fudge recipe dating from the late 19th or early 20th century.

## History of Fudge

It is also sometimes thought that the first batch of fudge was a result of an accidentally 'fudged' batch of caramels in which fudge required its name.

# Story of the Store Cupboard

## Story of the Store Cupboard

Kitchens have come an awfully long way since the early days of fudge making, as have the supplies stocked in pantries and larders. Before modern conveniences such as fridges and freezers, one of the biggest hurdles housewives had to overcome was the task of preserving, and it was no mean feat! It is hard to imagine a world without the convenience of modern kitchen appliances, and keeping food fresh was a daily challenge.

There are many simple preservation methods that can be carried out in the kitchen, without the use of modern conveniences. Salt can be used to cure meat and fish, and pickling can preserve vegetables. The drying of fruit, herbs and spices is especially useful, and can be used across a wide range of recipes.

## Story of the Store Cupboard

Along with some clever cooking, sugar was another natural preservative used by housewives to preserve a glut of seasonal produce. Scrumptious jams, chutneys, and confectionery were commonly made and stockpiled for the coming months.

Having a well-stocked larder was the mark of a good housewife, and before easy preservation and storage methods became commonplace, fudge would have been a welcome addition to the larder's shelves.

# Story of the Store Cupboard

## STAPLE INGREDIENTS

Now, let's take a little time to get to know the ingredients you will need to make fudge at home. You'll be very familiar with most of the ingredients listed in this book, but there may also be things that are new to you if you've not made fudge at home before.

Much like with your kitchen equipment, making sure you have the right supplies is very important before you get started. Here are a few fudge-making staples, with a little explanation:

# Story of the Store Cupboard

## Sugar

Until the late nineteenth century, sugar came in the form of sugarloaf. Granulated and cubed sugar came a little later so for a long while, if you wanted to use sugar you had to get to grips with a large sugarloaf cone. Housewives would buy their sugar in tall, conical loaves, and trim off what they needed with special iron sugar-cutters called sugar nips. If a recipe called for fine, granulated sugar, then a little elbow grease and a pestle and mortar would be enthusiastically employed!

## Story of the Store Cupboard

### Butter

Butter is made by churning milk, and is a staple ingredient in many a fudge recipe. Butter has been used for centuries, and is an all-round useful foodstuff to have in your store cupboard. Pleasingly, butter will keep without being refrigerated, unlike many other dairy products. The ease in which butter can be stored would have been especially appreciated in the days before modern conveniences such as refrigerators.

# Story of the Store Cupboard

## Milk and cream

Milk and cream are also important additions to fudge, and will give your confectionery a smooth consistency and rich taste. Before modern refrigeration methods, milk and cream were very difficult to store safely, as they go off when not kept cool. The milkman would have delivered milk and cream daily, and ensured it was kept cool while on his round by packing the bottles into shaved ice. Housewives would quickly store it in their ice boxes at home in the hope that they could keep the milk fresh until the next delivery.

# Story of the Store Cupboard

# Wartime Rationing

## Wartime Rationing

During the 1930s, the country's love affair with sugar came under attack. As World War II air raid sirens sounded throughout Britain's cities, a different war was being fought behind closed doors by the country's army of housewives. Trade routes to the UK were targeted during the war, and food supplies quickly dwindled. On 8 January 1940, bacon, butter and sugar were rationed by the government, followed in subsequent months by meat, tea, jam and much more.

Despite being armed with her government-issued ration book containing coupons for all rationed items, the average housewife's weekly shopping basket was suddenly much

# Wartime Rationing

lighter than before. Creating tasty and nutritious meals for the family became a real challenge for many.

Sugar became a very precious resource, and a thriving black market quickly sprung up as a result of the strict rationing. With legitimate supplies so very low, mothers had to be increasingly inventive in order to supply their children and husbands with sweet treats.

## Wartime Rationing

Many recipes for sweet substitutes were circulated during wartime Britain, with most ingeniously using the natural sugars from fruits and vegetables such as carrots and beetroot. Confectionery was a real treat, and sweets were rationed to 12oz per month, so anything a clever housewife could magic up in the kitchen was seen to be a real coup.

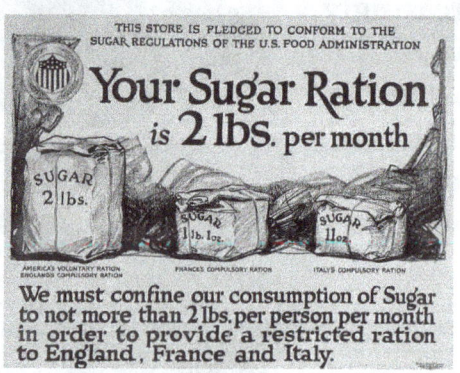

# Sourcing Your Supplies

## Sourcing Your Supplies

These days, you are lucky that you can make sure your pantry is stocked with all that you might need. Gone are the days of visiting a host of shops to get what you need. Without the convenience of large supermarkets, it could take a busy housewife the best part of the day to fill her shopping basket with supplies for the week from her local high street.

And with such an array of mod cons in the kitchen these days, storing ingredients and preparing sweet treats has never been easier. With a good selection of fudge-making basics in your store cupboard you can try a huge

## Sourcing Your Supplies

array of recipes, without the bother of having to go out shopping every time you want to get a batch of fudge bubbling on the stove.

Finding the best ingredients before you put your apron on and start cooking is important, as the lovelier your ingredients are, the lovelier your fudge will be. Look at the local produce on offer in your area. it is so often the case that the best things to eat are the things that grow locally, are in season, and haven't travelled a huge distance. Not only do these things taste better than their imported counterparts, but it is far kinder to the environment to use what is nearby.

## Sourcing Your Supplies

Perhaps you have a wonderful local greengrocer who can supply you with seasonal fruit, or a brilliant local health food shop where you can stock up on ingredients? Use your local suppliers and their expertise, as their knowledge will be rather useful to you while you are still getting to grips with the basics.

# Equipment

# Equipment

Now you should be feeling ready to get creative and start making your own fudge at home. The list of utensils and equipment you will need is not huge, but it is important you have the basics at your fingertips.

Firstly, you will need a large saucepan. A copper-bottomed jam boiler is perfect for this, as it will be designed to withstand very high cooking temperature of fudge, as well as be big enough to contain boiling sugar bubbles. A smaller saucepan will also be useful, as

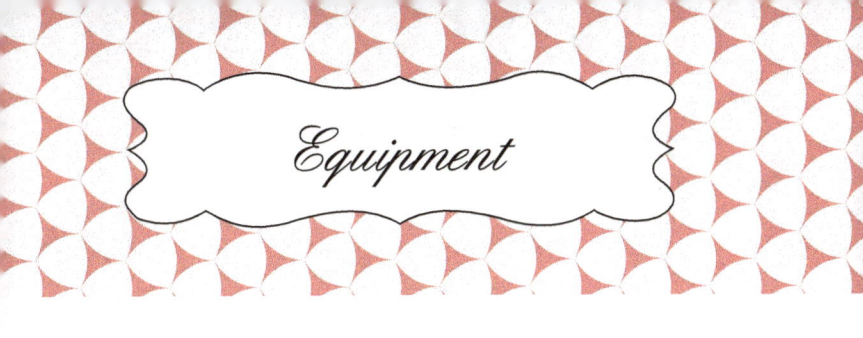

# Equipment

some recipes require the mixture to be cooked in two batches.

A wooden spoon for stirring your boiling sugar mixture will be essential, as plastic may not withstand the high temperature. You will also need a spatula or scraper for working your mixture. You must be careful working with the cooling mixture, and a good spatula is key to ensure you can safely work your fudge. A metal scraper is best, due to the high temperature of fudge mixture.

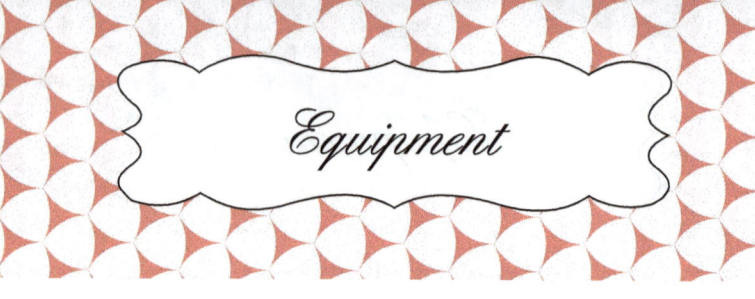

# Equipment

Working your mixture will also require the use of a marble slab, or work surface. A portion of old marble washstand is perfect for this, and you can often buy them relatively cheaply from antique markets. If you cannot find a marble washstand, a thick marble or glass chopping board will be just as effective. Storing your board in the fridge before use is

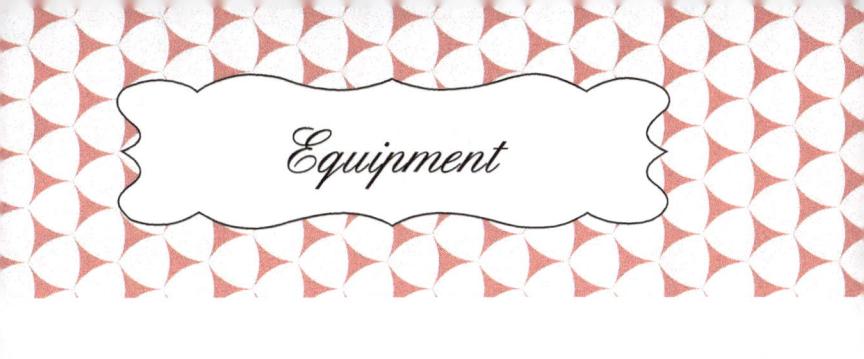

# Equipment

helpful, and will help cool the fudge mixture as you work it.

However, working your fudge mixture is not essential. It is perfectly possible to simply beat your fudge mixture in the pan and pour into a buttered baking tin to cool. A large mixing bowl and a good whisk may also come in handy if the recipes requires beaten egg whites.

# Equipment

## EQUIPMENT CHECKLIST

**A** small saucepan

*

**Measuring** cups and scales

*

**Sugar** thermometer

*

**Wooden** spoon

*

**Bench** scraper or spatula

*

**Marble** slab, or other heatsafe board

*

**Shallow** baking tin

*

**Greaseproof** paper

*

**Sharp** knife

*

**Large** mixing bowl

*

**Whisk**

# Measurements

# Measurements

In the most part, measurements in the recipes in this book will be in cups. A small coffee cup is the best kind to use, and make sure you use the same cup to measure all your ingredients.

You may not be familiar with using cups to measure ingredients but they are a quick and easy way of portioning the rather large quantities of sugar, that some fudge recipes call for.

Cups have been used in cookery for generations, after an American culinary expert called Fanny Farmer introduced them as a standardised form of measurement in recipes.

# Measurements

Accuracy and consistency are very important in any recipe, especially for fudge, so Fanny's work was rather groundbreaking at the time.

Fanny published her best-known cookery book 'The Boston Cooking-School Cook Book' in 1896, and it has been used by generations of keen cooks ever since. Fanny introduced these new standardised measurements by stressing the importance of levelling off the cup as you measure. It may seem insignificant, but before her clever intervention, cooks had to make do with instructions such as 'a large dash', 'a goodly pinch', and even 'butter the size of an egg'. Rather amusing, but a little inconsistent, don't you agree?

# Measurements

**Of course, you don't have to use cups. This table is a handy tool if you need to convert cups into other amounts.**

| 1 cup | 8 fluid ounces | ½ pint | 237 ml |
| --- | --- | --- | --- |
| 2 cups | 16 fluid ounces | 1 pint | 474 ml |
| 4 cups | 32 fluid ounces | 1 quart | 946 ml |
| 2 pints | 32 fluid ounces | 1 quart | 0.946 l |
| 4 quarts | 128 fluid ounces | 1 gallon | 3.784 l |

# Temperature

## Temperature

Being able to gauge the temperature of your mixture as it cooks is essential when you're making fudge at home. Just a few degrees over or under your desired temperature will result in a very different final product, so it is important that you carefully monitor your fudge mixture as it cooks.

Boiling sugar may seem like quite a demanding task. One must be mindful of safety at all times as it is easy to burn yourself on the cooking mixture. The change in temperature can often be rather rapid so it is very important that you heat the mixture gradually, to avoid a sudden change in temperature.

# Temperature

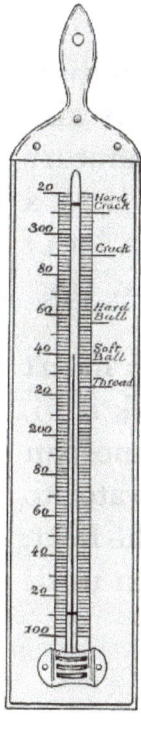

Many of the recipes in this book are classic recipes which have been used in countless kitchens, by generations of cooks.

The temperatures stated in the recipes in this book will be in Fahrenheit, as this is the original form of measuring temperature. The metric system which uses the Celsius scale took some time to be introduced internationally, and Fahrenheit is still widely used to this day.

# Temperature

A thermometer is the safest way to monitor the temperature of boiling sugar. It is also the easiest way to gauge the exact temperature of your cooking fudge mixture, so it is a good idea to use one until you have a lot of experience working with boiling sugar.

If you have a new thermometer which hasn't been used before, make sure you break it in. You can do this by placing it into a saucepan of cold water, and then heating the water to boiling point. Remove the pan from the heat, but leave the thermometer in the pan until the water has cooled.

# Temperature

## Tip

After use, plunge your thermometer into warm water and wipe with a soft cloth.

Remember to do this rather promptly after you have used it, as the boiled sweet mixture will cool, and be very difficult to clean off later.

# Temperature

## THE DROP TEST

These days we are lucky that sugar thermometers are readily available and are relatively cheap to buy. This was not always the case. Before the introduction of this nifty household tool, another ingenious method had to be employed to test the temperature of fudge mixture as it cooked.

This age old method is called The Drop Test.

By carefully dropping a little mixture into some cold water, you can gauge the stage the mixture is at by the type of mass the mixture forms. Once mastered, this rather ingenious little skill is a failsafe way of monitoring

# Temperature

your fudge mixture, and is a truly authentic fudge-making method. If you choose to use the drop test method whilst making your fudge, do be mindful of the dangers of boiling sugar. You don't want a nasty burn, so be very careful when testing your mixture.

Most of the recipes in this book will state to heat the mixture to soft ball stage, which is around 240°F. If the fudge mixture forms a soft ball when tested in cold water then you have reached the correct temperature.

Have a look at the table we have provided for more information on regulating the temperature of your fudge mixture without a thermometer. This should give you a good idea of what to look out for at each stage of cooking.

# The Drop Test

| Stage | Temperature | Uses |
|---|---|---|
| Thread - Forms a thin liquid thread | 110°C to 112 °C (230 to 234 °F) | Sugar Syrups |
| Soft ball - Forms a soft flexible ball that can be flattened. | 112°C to 116 °C (234 to 241 °F) | Fudge, pralines, fondant and butter creams |
| Firm ball - Forms a firm ball that will hold its shape but is still malleable | 118°C to 120 °C (244 to 248 °F) | Caramel Candies |
| Hard ball - Forms thick threads from spoon and creates a hard ball that will hold its shape | 121 to 130 °C (250 to 266 °F) | Nougat, marshmallows, gummies, and divinity |
| Soft crack - Forms firm flexible threads | 132°C to 143 °C (270 to 289 °F) | salt water taffy |
| Hard crack - Forms hard brittle threads that snap easily | 146°C to 154 °C (295 to 309 °F) | toffee, brittles, hard candy, and lollipops |
| Clear liquid - Liquid will begin to change colour. Colour ranges from golden brown to amber | 160 °C (320 °F) | caramelised sugar, caramel |
| Brown liquid - Liquid will begin to change colour. Colour ranges from golden brown to amber | 170 °C (338 °F) | caramelised sugar, caramel |

# Techniques

# Techniques

## WORKING

Very often fudge recipes will require you to work the cooling mixture, which is a traditional fudge-making technique. It is a straightforward technique, and is an effective way to blend ingredients as well as shape your fudge. Working your fudge mixture by hand also gives a wonderfully smooth creamy consistency to your final product. Once you have mastered this basic technique you'll be able to make an impressive array of fudge at home in your kitchen.

After you take the saucepan of fudge mixture off the heat, leave the mixture to cool slightly for a while or until under 120°F. Now, it is

# Techniques

time to wash your hands, put on an apron, and roll up your sleeves. You'll need a little patience and a spot of elbow grease for this. Wearing a pair of latex gloves will also help protect your hands from the heat.

Once cooled, carefully pour the mixture onto a lightly oiled marble slab or board. A portion of old washstand or work surface is perfect for this, although any heat-safe surface will suffice.

Next, with a bench scraper, begin folding the fudge mixture onto itself repeatedly, working it into the required shape. Keep scraping and folding, especially if you are additional ingredients or flavouring into your mixture at this stage. Have a little patience, and repeat this process until the mixture holds its shape.

# Techniques

## BEATING

It is well worth noting that working your fudge mixture is not essential. If you wish, you can simply beat your fudge mixture thoroughly in the pan before carefully pouring it into the buttered tin. In the absence of working, beating the mixture will create the same smooth, creamy consistency which is essential to making successful fudge.

A wooden spoon is best for beating fudge mixture, as plastic utensils may not withstand the hot temperature of the mixture. Be careful when beating the mixture, as it will be very hot, and sugar burns can be painful.

# Techniques

After removing your pan from the heat, leave the mixture to stand for a few minutes, until the bubbling has abated. The mixture should be no more than 120°F when you begin beating. Any warmer, and the mixture may become grainy.

Start by scraping the edges of your saucepan to incorporate the all of the mixture, and briskly stir the mixture until you can feel it thickening. When the fudge mixture begins to thicken, increase the speed of your stirring until you are beating the mixture. Finish by

## Techniques

stirring the mixture slowly and steadily, to get rid of any small bubbles you may have created by beating. Now the mixture is ready to be poured into a buttered tin, and can be marked into squares when cool.

Now, you can take a well-earned rest.

# Traditional Favourites

The first section of recipes is dedicated to traditional old-time fudge recipes that have been used for decades. They range from simple recipes, to more indulgent classics. You are sure to find a fudge for any occasion among these traditional favourites.

# Simple Fudge

Here's a wonderful recipe for homemade fudge to start you off. This recipe is very straightforward, and is a great place to start if you're a fudge-making beginner. You can use this classic recipe as a base to which you can add creative combinations of your favourite dried fruit and nuts.

# Simple Fudge

**3 cups sugar**
**1 cup milk**
**1 tsp vanilla extract**

**1.** Caramelise one cup of sugar. **2.** Heat the milk and the remaining sugar in a separate pan, and when it's boiling add the caramel sugar. **3.** Stir constantly until it registers 240°F, or forms a soft ball when tested in cold water. **4.** Remove from heat and add the vanilla extract. **5.** Beat until creamy and pour into buttered tins.

## Chocolate Fudge

Chocolate is a great addition to fudge, and has long been added to classic fudge recipes. Try this recipe for chocolate fudge which includes a hint of vanilla for a distinctively sweet finish.

# Chocolate Fudge

**2 ½ cups sugar**
**3 tbsp butter**
**½ cup milk**
**1 tbsp glucose**
**½ cup cocoa**
**1 tsp vanilla extract**

**1.** Put the sugar, glucose, butter, cocoa and milk into a saucepan and stir until it reaches 240°F, or forms a soft ball when tested in cold water. **2.** Remove the pan from the heat and stir in the vanilla extract. Allow the mixture to cool to about 120ºF. **3.** Carefully pour the mixture onto a marble slab, or other heatsafe work surface. **4.** With a bench scraper or spatula, begin folding the mixture onto itself repeatedly, working it into the centre of your work surface. **5.** Keep scraping and folding until the mixture starts to hold its shape. **6.** When firm, cut into squares or bars.

# Sultana & Nut Fudge

Dried fruit and nuts have long been used to create sticky, sweet treats. The very earliest forms of confectionery from the middle ages consisted of fruits and nuts bound together by a sticky, sweet substance like honey. Dried fruit and nuts are the perfect additions to many a fudge recipe. All nuts work well, but make sure you chop them quite finely so they mix well with your fudge mixture. This fantastic recipe for sultana and nut fudge has the perfect blend of fruit and nuts giving it a fantastic crunchy texture.

# Sultana & Nut Fudge

**3 tbsp butter**
**3 tbsp molasses**
**1 ½ cups sugar**
**3 oz chocolate**
**½ cup milk**
**½ cup chopped walnuts**
**1 cup sultanas**
**1 tsp vanilla extract**
**1 tsp orange extract**

**1.** Put the butter sugar, molasses, chocolate, sugar and milk into a saucepan and heat until the mixture reaches 240°F, or forms a soft ball when tested in cold water. **2.** Add the chopped nuts, sultanas and extracts and remove the pan from the heat. **3.** Allow the mixture to cool to about 120°F. **4.** Carefully pour the mixture onto a marble slab, or other heatsafe work surface. **5.** With a bench scraper or spatula, begin folding the mixture onto itself repeatedly, working it into the centre of your work surface. **6.** Keep scraping and folding until the mixture starts to hold its shape. **7.** When firm, cut into squares or bars.

# Christmas Fudge

Christmas is a perfect time to get creative in the kitchen. Fudge is popular all over the world, and in America it is traditionally made and enjoyed from Thanksgiving to Easter. Handmade fudge makes a great gift, and it is easy to make large batches at a time. You can add crystallised fruit to your fudge mixture for a pop of festive colour.

## Christmas Fudge

2 cups sugar
1 cup cream
2 tbsp butter
1 tsp vanilla extract
1 square melted chocolate
1 tbsp dried chopped cranberries
1 tbsp chopped angelica
½ cup chopped nuts
Dash of brandy (optional)

**1.** Put the sugar, cream, and butter into a saucepan and boil for half an hour, stirring constantly. **2.** Add the chocolate to the mixture and bring the mixture to the boil. **3.** Remove the pan from the heat and beat until the mixture is creamy, then add the vanilla extract, the fruit and nuts. (and brandy, if using) **4.** Allow the mixture to cool to about 120°F. **5.** Carefully pour the mixture onto a marble slab, or other heatsafe work surface. **6.** With a bench scraper or spatula, begin folding the mixture onto itself repeatedly, working it into the centre of your work surface. **7.** Keep scraping and folding until the mixture starts to hold its shape. **8.** When firm, cut into squares or bars.

# Angel Food Fudge

This wonderful recipe for angel food fudge was popular in Victorian times, and a version is included in the 1861 book by Isabella Beeton, 'Book of Household Management'. The Victorians loved the use of milk, cream and honey in their cooking, and thought these ingredients to be very nutritious. This recipe includes clear honey for a wonderfully sweet fudge which is light in colour.

# Angel Food Fudge

⅔ cup clear honey
2 ¼ cup sugar
⅔ cup cold water
½ tsp cream of tartar
2 egg whites
2 tsp orange flower water
1 cup chopped, blanched almonds

---

**1.** In a heavy-bottomed saucepan, stir the honey, sugar and water over a low heat. **2.** When the sugar has dissolved, add the cream of tartar, and boil until the mixture reaches 240°F, or until the mixture forms a soft ball when tested in cold water. **3.** Beat the egg whites until they form stiff peaks, then gradually add the sugar solution to the egg whites a little at a time, stirring continuously until it has been incorporated. **4.** When the mixture becomes stiff, stir in the orange flower water and the almonds. **5.** Carefully pour the mixture into a buttered tin, and mark into squares when cool.

# Divinity Fudge

Divinity fudge is another classic recipe, which dates back to the early 1900s. The name is said to come from the exclamation of one of its first testers. "Divine!", it was said to be described as, and the name stuck. It is believed that divinity became popular at this time, as one of its ingredients, corn syrup, was becoming more readily available than it had been previously. This traditional recipe for divinity fudge substitutes the corn syrup with golden syrup, but if you can source corn syrup, feel free to use it, for a truly authentic take on this recipe.

## Divinity Fudge

**12 oz caster sugar**
**⅔ cup water**
**2 tbsp golden syrup**
**2 egg whites**
**1 cup chopped walnuts**
**½ tsp vanilla essence**

**1.** Beat the egg whites in a bowl until they form stiff peaks. **2.** In a heavy-bottomed saucepan, stir the sugar and the water over a low heat, until the mixture reaches 238ºF, or until the mixture forms a soft ball when tested in cold water. **3.** Pour half of the boiling syrup into the beaten egg whites, and leave the remaining syrup to cook until it reaches 250ºF, or until the mixture forms a hard ball when tested in cold water. **4.** Add the remaining syrup to the egg whites, and continue beating. **5.** When the mixture begins to stiffen, add the walnuts and the vanilla essence. **6.** Carefully pour the mixture into a buttered tin and mark into squares when cool.

# Classic College Recipes

The origins of fudge have been tracked back to a group women who studied at colleges in America. It is unusual that such a popular foodstuff was invented by women, as at the time of creation, most new discovers, food and otherwise, were being made by men. This next batch of recipes are all college favourites, and have been made by students and non-students alike for decades.

## Vassar College Fudge

This recipe is one of the original recipes for fudge which came from Vassar college in the United States of America. You can follow in the footsteps of Emelyn Battersby and create your very own Vassar College fudge using the classic recipe below.

# Vassar College Fudge

**2 cups granulated white sugar**
**1 cup cream**
**2 oz unsweetened chocolate, chopped**
**1 tbsp butter**

**1.** Combine the sugar and cream in a saucepan and stir over a moderate heat. When this becomes very hot, add the chocolate. **2.** Stir constantly until the mixture reaches 240°F, or forms a soft ball when tested in cold water. **3.** Remove the pan from the heat and gently stir in the butter. **4.** Beat until the mixture starts to thicken and carefully pour the mixture into a buttered tin. **5.** Cut into pieces before the fudge hardens completely.

# Sorority Fudge

Here is another college-inspired recipe for fudge which you could try. This one contains a few more ingredients, including orange extract which will give your fudge an unmistakably zingy flavour.

## Sorority Fudge

½ cup butter
1 cup brown sugar
1 cup granulated sugar
½ cup cream
3 tbsp molasses
2 oz grated chocolate
1 ½ tsp orange extract
4 tbsp chopped angelica

**1.** Mix the sugar, molasses and cream in a saucepan then add the butter. **2.** Bring to the boil for three minutes, stirring rapidly. **3.** Add the chocolate and boil for five minutes stirring quickly, then more slowly. **4.** Remove the pan from the heat, as the orange extract and angelica. **5.** Beat until the mixture thickens, then carefully pour into buttered tins.

# Smith College Fudge

Here is another classic college recipe for fudge for you to try out. This recipe originates from Smith College in the United States of America, and is another of the very earliest recorded recipes for fudge. A hint of vanilla and chocolate give this confectionery a lovely sweetness.

## Smith College Fudge

1/4 cup butter
1 cup sugar
1 cup brown sugar
1/4 cup molasses
1/2 cup cream
2 squares chocolate, chopped fine
1 1/2 tsp vanilla

**1.** Melt the butter in a heavy saucepan. Add in sugar, brown sugar, molasses and cream. **2.** Bring to a boil, and continue to boil for 2 ½ minutes, stirring constantly. **3.** Add the chocolate to the mixture, and boil for another 5 minutes. **4.** Remove the pan from the heat and add the vanilla. **5.** Beat until the mixture thickens. **6.** Carefully pour the mixture into a buttered tin and cut into squares as it cools.

## Classic Twists

Now here's a section dedicated to those fudge recipes which have a little extra something added. Whether you are looking to try out liqueur, or marshmallows in your fudge recipe, you are sure to find something to tickle your among these classics, which each have a twist.

## Coffee Fudge

Coffee is a great addition to fudge. The strong, bitter flavour of coffee cuts through the sweetness of fudge, and will give your mixture a wonderfully dark and rich colour. Fresh coffee will work best in this recipe, but a strong cup of instant coffee will also suffice.

## Coffee Fudge

**2 cups sugar**
**1 cup strong coffee**
**1 tbsp butter**
**1 cup pecan nuts, chopped**
**1 tsp almond extract**

---

**1.** Mix the sugar, coffee and butter together in a saucepan and heat, stirring all the time, until the mixture reaches 240°F, or forms a soft ball when tested in cold water. **2.** Remove the pan from the heat, add the almond extract and beat until the mixture begins to stiffen. **3.** Pour the fudge mixture over the chopped nuts in a buttered tin, and mark into squares when cool.

# Rum & Raisin Fudge

Liqueur works perfectly in fudge, complementing the sweet and creamy taste. Liqueur was first added to sweets in the late 1930s by a confectioner from Kentucky named Ruth Hanly Booe. She liked to use bourbon in her recipes, but you can add a large splash of any liqueur to your fudge mixture during the final stir for a truly indulgent treat. Liqueur-laced fudge makes a wonderful gift for adults, and is also the perfect after-dinner offering.

## Rum & Raisin Fudge

**4 cups sugar**
**1 can evaporated milk**
**1 cup butter**
**½ cup chocolate pieces**
**1 pint cream**
**1 dash of rum**
**1 cup chopped walnuts**
**1 cup chopped pecans**

**1.** Mix the sugar, milk and butter in a saucepan and heat until the mixture reaches 240°F, or forms a soft ball when tested in cold water. **2.** Remove the pan from the heat and add chocolate pieces, cream, rum, walnuts and pecans. **3.** Stir the mixture until the chocolate is well-blended, Remove the pan from the heat and allow the mixture to cool to about 120ºF. **4.** Carefully pour the mixture onto a marble slab, or other heatsafe work surface. **5.** With a bench scraper or spatula, begin folding the mixture onto itself repeatedly, working it into the centre of your work surface. **6.** Keep scraping and folding until the mixture starts to hold its shape. **7.** When firm, cut into squares or bars.

# Peanut Butter Fudges

Peanut butter was first made in the late 1800s. Dr. John Harvey Kellogg, the man credited with the invention of corn flakes, patented a 'Process of Preparing Nut Meal' in 1895 and used peanuts. Kellogg was interested in the health benefits of peanuts and found peanut butter to be an effective way for a patient to easily consume a large amount of protein.

Peanut butter is also a popular addition to a range of confectionery and is an ingenious way to add texture to your fudge. You can add chopped nuts to the tin before pouring the mixture in for a more coarse texture.

# Peanut Butter Fudges

**2 heaped tbsp peanut butter**
**½ cup milk**
**2 cups sugar**
**1 tsp ginger extract**

**1.** Put the sugar, milk and peanut butter into a saucepan and stir until the mixture boils for exactly five minutes. **2.** Remove the pan from the heat, add the ginger extract and stir until the mixture thickens. **3.** Pour into a buttered tin and cut into squares when cool.

# Marshmallow Fudge

The use of marshmallow to make a sweets dates back to ancient Egypt, where the recipe involved extracting sap from the marshmallow plant and mixing it with nuts and honey. The sap from this plant is said to have healing properties, and is an age-old remedy for sore throats. Try this simple recipe for marshmallow fudge, which also includes nuts to give your fudge a wonderful crunch.

# Marshmallow Fudge

2 cups brown sugar
1 cups maple sugar
1 cup water
1 pinch cream of tartar
1 tbsp chopped pecans
2 cups marshmallows

**1.** Dissolve the sugar in the water in a saucepan, then add the cream of tartar and boil without stirring until the mixture reaches 240°F, or forms a soft ball when tested in cold water. **2.** Remove the pan from the heat, and add the marshmallows and the pecans. **3.** Allow the mixture to cool to about 120ºF. **4.** Carefully pour the mixture onto a marble slab, or other heatsafe work surface. **5.** With a bench scraper or spatula, begin folding the mixture onto itself repeatedly, working it into the centre of your work surface. **6.** Keep scraping and folding until the mixture starts to hold its shape. **7.** When firm, cut into squares or bars.

# Wartime Recipes

This next selection of recipes would have been popular during wartime rationing. During the war, housewives had to get rather creative in order to make sweet treats without using sugar, which was incredibly scarce. Learning how to harness the natural sugars in vegetables meant a huge range of cakes and confections could be made despite meagre rations.

## Carrot Fudge

Carrot was an ingenious and effective substitute, and many wartime recipes for cakes and confectionery included carrot. Here is a popular and simple wartime fudge recipe which uses carrot.

# Carrot Fudge

**6 Carrots**
**1 gelatin leaf**
**Orange essence**

**1.** Grate the carrots and boil them gently in a saucepan for 10 minutes. **2.** Add the orange essence to the mixture. **3.** Melt the gelatin leaf and add it to the mixture. **4.** Cook quickly for a few minutes, stirring constantly. **5.** Spoon into a flat dish and cut into cubes when set.

# Mashed Potato Fudge

Here's another rather unusual recipe for fudge which has a surprising vegetable base. Potato is a surprisingly good addition to fudge, as the starch in the root vegetables add a wonderful thickness to the mixture. As potato has a very subtle flavour as well as lots of natural sugar, it is possible to use mashed or riced cooked potato in sweet recipes and drastically cut down on the amount of sugar you need to use.

# Mashed Potato Fudge

3 oz unsweetened chocolate
½ cup water
1 tbsp butter
¼ cup mashed potato
½ teaspoon vanilla essence
2 cups caster sugar

**1.** In a heavy-bottomed saucepan heat the water on a low heat. Chop the chocolate and add this and the butter to the pan. **2.** Stir in the potato and vanilla essence. **3.** Add the sugar gradually, one spoonful at a time. When mixture becomes difficult to stir, turn it out on a marble slab or lightly oiled board and work in more sugar with your hands. **4.** Press the mixture into a buttered baking tin, and mark into squares when cool.

# Honey Fudge

Using honey is a great way to make fudge without the usual large quantities of sugar as it has almost exactly the same sweetness ounce for ounce as regular granulated sugar. Honey has been a popular addition to lots of confectionery for centuries, although has been relied on less since it became possible to acquire sugar more cheaply. This recipe would have been very handy during wartime sugar rationing, and is a great way to use and preserve the zesty peels of citrus fruits.

# Honey Fudge

**10 tbsp honey**
**10 tbsp cream**
**1 pinch of salt**
**½ tsp lemon juice**
**1 handful dried cherries**
**1 tbsp chopped lemon zest**

**1.** In a saucepan, bring the cream and honey slowly to boiling point, then cook for six minutes when the mixture begins to boil, or until a white line appears around the edge when the mixture is stirred. **2.** Remove the pan from the heat, stir in the salt and the lemon juice. **3.** Arrange the cherries on a buttered tin and pour the fudge mixture over. **4.** Sprinkle the chopped peel over the cooling mixture.

If you would have your Fudge the kind that really can't be beaten, Then you must Beat it hard & Beat it before it can be eaten. And strange it is, but very true — the harder that you beat it the Better Fudge you will admit it is for those who eat it.

# The Etiquette of Serving

# The Etiquette of Serving

Finding new and interesting recipes to impress dinner party guests could be a daunting prospect for a hostess, but offering carefully crafted homemade fudge to guests at the end of the evening was seen to be an elegant touch.

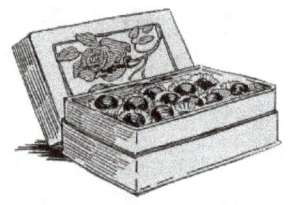

# The Etiquette of Serving

Traditionally, fudge would have been served at the end of supper, perhaps to accompany coffee. A selection of fudge was placed in a pretty dish and offered to guests. A classic recipe containing vanilla and nuts made a very dainty alternative to dessert after a heavy meal.

# The Etiquette of Serving

Today, you can still find beautiful antique glass and china dishes specifically for serving confectionery. Some have lids but some are made without lids and are perfect for serving your fudge to guests at the dinner table. Glass dishes are perfect for displaying your hard work, and you can add a linen napkin or paper doily to your dish before filling with fudge if you prefer.

# Gifts

# Gifts

There is nothing nicer than a handmade gift, and what better way to make the most of your new-found fudge-making skills than to give it to a loved one as a present.

Homemade fudge makes the perfect Christmas or birthday gift, and you can even add your loved ones' favourite ingredients to the recipe for a truly personal touch.

# Gifts

Why not try adding a splash of liqueur to a batch of your fudge for a tremendously indulgent treat for adults?

Fold your fudge into greaseproof paper to make sure it doesn't stick together and carefully wrap your gift. Small cardboard boxes from craft shops are also perfect this, and can be wrapped in festive paper, too.

We hope you have enjoyed this little book about the wonderful world of making fudge. We hope we have we have been able to provide a wealth of useful and practical information that can be passed on again, so that these invaluable skills will not be lost.

Credits and Attributions

Cover Image, Title page and Page 4 - This work is a derivative of "1956-Electrolux" is copyright © October 17, 2009 James Vaughn, x-ray delta one, made available on Flickr under Creative Commons Attribution 2.0 Generic (CC BY 2.0) http://www.flickr.com/photos/x-ray_delta_one/4017899831/sizes/l/in/faves-90808113@N04/

Page 10 - This work is a derivative of "It's All You Need" is Copyright © 1950 Posted by noluck_boston, made available on vintage-ads.livejournal.com http://vintage-ads.livejournal.com/tag/cleaning

Page 13 - This work is a derivative of "Waste Not want not" is Copyright © 1914 Canadian Food Board, Hamilton [Ontario, Canada] : Howell Lith., made available onwww.loc.gov/ under The Public Domain Licence http://www.loc.gov/pictures/item/2005696499/

Page 18 - This work is a derivative of "whenmotherletsus inside page" is Copyright © 1915 New York, Moffat, Yard and company, made available on Archive under The Public Domain Licence http://archive.org/details/whenmotherletsus00bach

Page 21 - This work is a derivative of "Do with less, so they'll have enough! Rationing gives you your fair share" is Copyright © 1943, posted by United States. Office of War Information. Division of Public Inquiries, made available on UNT Digital Library under The Public Domain Licence http://digital.library.unt.edu/ark:/67531/metadc538/?q=Rationing

Page 22 - This work is a derivative of "Your Sugar Ration 1917 - ca. 1919" is Copyright ©1917 U.S. Food Administration. Educational Division. Advertising Section, made available on Wikimedia under The Public Domain Licence http://commons.wikimedia.org/wiki/File:%22This_Store_is_pledged_to_conform_to_the_Sugar_Regulations_of_the_Food_Administration._Your_Sugar_Ration_is_2lbs._per_mo_-_NARA_-_512525.jpg

Page 26 - This work is a derivative of "Narragansett Electric Co.'s Fat and Grease – Pass the Ammunition (1943)" is Copyright © 1943 posted by Ginevra, midniterose, made available on vintage-ads.livejournal.com http://vintage-ads.livejournal.com/tag/ww2%20rationing

Page 28 - This work is a derivative of "Pg. 94, COPPER CANDY LADLE. Fig 7" is Copyright © 1896, The Candy Maker's Guide, by Fletcher Manufacturing Company made available on Gutenburg under The Public Domain Licence http://www.gutenberg.org/files/30293/30293-h/30293-h.htm

Page 29 - This work is a derivative of "Pg. 94, COPPER CANDY LADLE. Fig 8" is Copyright © 1896, The Candy Maker's Guide, by Fletcher Manufacturing Company made available on Gutenburg under The Public Domain Licence http://www.gutenberg.org/files/30293/30293-h/30293-h.htm

Page 30 Page 31 Page 32 Page 34 - This work is a derivative of "whenmotherletsus pg 17" is Copyright © 1915 New York, Moffat, Yard and company, made available on Archive under The Public Domain Licence http://archive.org/details/whenmotherletsus00bach

Page 32 - This work is a derivative of "LIFE Dec 12, 1955 hamilton watches christmas spread" is Copyright © 1955, posted by Jocelmeow, made available on vintage-ads.livejournal.com http://vintage-ads.livejournal.com/tag/1945

Page 35 - This work is a derivative of "Maxwell House Coffee (1950) " is Copyright © 1950 posted by, pikkewyntjie made available on vintage-ads.livejournal.com http://vintage-ads.livejournal.com/tag/1950

Page 39 - This work is a derivative of "whenmotherletsus pg 18" is Copyright © 1915 New York, Moffat, Yard and company, made available on Archive under The Public Domain Licence http://archive.org/details/whenmotherletsus00bach

Page 41 - This work is a derivative of "Diced Cream of America Co., 1949" is Copyright © 1949, posted by Man Writing Slash (write_light), made available on vintage-ads.livejournal.com http://vintage-ads.livejournal.com/tag/1949

Page 49 - This work is a derivative of "whenmotherletsus pg 24" is Copyright © 1915 New York, Moffat, Yard and company, made available on Archive under The Public Domain Licence http://archive.org/details/whenmotherletsus00bach

Page 50 - This work is a derivative of "Wright's Coal Tar Soap Ad, Child asleep near mother, 1922" is Copyright © 1922 Wright's Coal Tar Soap made available on wikimedia and flickr under The Public Domain Licence http://commons.wikimedia.org/wiki/File:Wright's_Coal_Tar_Soap,_1922.jpg

Page 94 - This work is a derivative of "whenmotherletsus pg 26" is Copyright © 1915 New York, Moffat, Yard and company, made available on Archive under The Public Domain Licence http://archive.org/details/whenmotherletsus00bach

Page 95 - This work is a derivative of "Vintage ChinaTaken from Mrs Beetons Everyday Cookery & Housekeeping" is Copyright © 1893, posted by tiffany terry, libertygrace0 made available on flickr under Creative commons Attribution 2.0 Generic (CC BY 2.0) http://www.flickr.com/photos/35168673@N03/4392797084/in/set-72157627296287304

Page 96 - This work is a derivative of "Three legged glass dish" is Copyright © January 27, 2012 , Joanna Bourne, made available on flickr under Creative commons Attribution 2.0 Generic (CC BY 2.0) http://www.flickr.com/photos/66992990@N00/6773469145/sizes/l/

Page 98 - This work is a derivative of "Tiffany Blue" is Copyright © May 18, 2008, Jill Clardy, made available on flickr under Creative commons Attribution 2.0 Generic (CC BY 2.0) http://www.flickr.com/photos/jillclardy/2523850043/

Page 99 - This work is a derivative of "UH-OH - Oreo / Nabisco, 1951" is Copyright © 1951, posted by Man Writing Slash (write_light), made available on vintage-ads.livejournal.com http://vintage-ads.livejournal.com/tag/1919

www.ingramcontent.com/pod-product-compliance
Lightning Source LLC
Chambersburg PA
CBHW050113170426
43198CB00014B/2566